Collins

EXTREME SURVIVAL

CONTENTS

Ple...
on or b...
Renew or...
www.boroug...poole.com/librar...

D0298941

INTRODUCTION

Most days, everything goes well. We get up, we go to school or work, we eat, we do our homework (maybe), we go to bed.

This book is about the days when things *didn't* go to plan for someone.

The days when things went *badly* wrong.

The days when people found themselves in a fight for survival. When they had to make choices that decided whether they lived or died.

Lost walkers survive by eating spiders

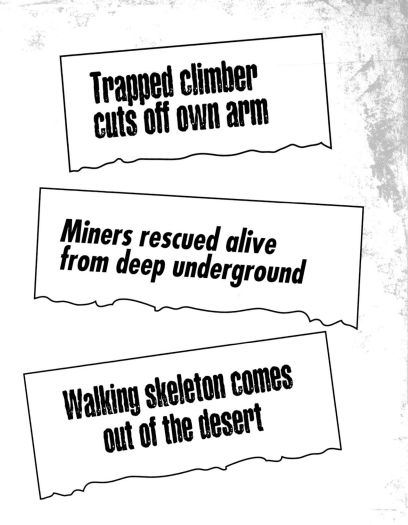

Trapped climber cuts off own arm

Miners rescued alive from deep underground

Walking skeleton comes out of the desert

Most of us live in safe places, where everything is under control. Extreme survival skills are needed when things go out of control or when we dare to leave that safety and head into the wilderness.

This book is about surviving in extreme situations.

- Sometimes it's the **landscape** that is extreme: mountains covered in ice, or tropical jungles.

- Sometimes it's the **climate** that causes problems: the heat and lack of water in desert areas, or the deadly cold and bone-chilling winds near the North and South Poles.

- Sometimes an accident is to blame: a plane crashes, a storm sinks a ship, or a building collapses.

> **landscape** type of countryside
> **climate** the usual type of weather in an area

Have you heard of either of these films? They are both based on true stories.

Some survival stories are well known.

Have you heard about Aron Ralston, who cut off his own arm with a penknife? Or about mountaineer Joe Simpson, who crawled to safety with a shattered leg?

This book has some true survival stories – and some survival tips that might just help you one day.

Rules of survival

Surviving usually involves staying alive until someone rescues you.

There are five key things.

1. Food

You can go for quite a long time without food, but you will need to eat to keep your strength up.

2. Water

Without water you won't last long. Use what you have carefully and try to find more.

3. Shelter

You'll need to find or build a shelter if you're going to be in one place for very long, particularly overnight. The weather can be a big problem.

4. Courage

You'll need to keep going when things might seem hopeless. Survivors are usually the ones who keep going when others give up.

5. Attracting attention

Make a fire or use a shiny object to reflect the sun. You might need to make a noise if you are trapped underground or under a building that has fallen down.

Water is vital for survival.

Survival tips

- Have a plan, but always be ready to adapt it.
  If something doesn't work, don't give up.
  Try something else instead.

- Don't let your body get too cold or hot.
  Cover up or strip off if you need to, but light
  clothes in the hot sun will help against sunburn.

- Water and food are important, but never eat
  or drink anything you're not sure about.

- Take some simple equipment – a length
  of cord, a knife, perhaps a fishing hook.
  It could save your life.

- You may need to attract the attention of a searching helicopter. A mirror that reflects sunlight, or a white cloth, would work well. Tie it to the end of a stick and wave it slowly.

- You are a very small person in a very big landscape. Make your sign as big as you can.

- Above all, don't stop exploring – when you're old, you'll be more disappointed by the things you didn't do than the ones you did!

Some more ideas for a survival kit: compass, penknife, whistle and torch

SURVIVING THE COLD

In extremely cold places, it is important to know the 30–30–30 rule. When the temperature drops to −30° Fahrenheit, in a 30 miles per hour wind, your flesh will start to freeze in just 30 seconds.

Forget your gloves when you go outside and you could lose your fingers!

The wind makes cold temperatures feel even colder. This is called "wind chill".

DID YOU KNOW?

Mittens keep your hands warmer than gloves. Do you know why?

The answer is on page 48.

Sir Ranulph Fiennes

Even great explorers sometimes get into trouble. Sir Ranulph Fiennes lost part of the fingers on his left hand after he got frostbite while trying to reach the North Pole on foot in 2000. His sledge fell through the ice and he took off his glove to drag it out.

Sir Ranulph Fiennes

… and his frostbitten fingers

SURVIVING WITHOUT WATER

Without water, you will probably die within a week – or faster in extreme heat.

Your body loses water all the time, through breathing and sweating, for example.

Water can be found in most places, but you need to know how to get to it. Keep a look-out for birds or insects, which will be near water, or look under stones where a little water might collect.

There may also be water deep underground, or inside a plant. Cacti may look tempting, but only some types hold water that is safe to drink. If you're going to a desert, it's a good idea to find out which ones they are.

You can always drink your own wee, although you'll probably have to be really thirsty to do that!

This desert landscape looks dry, but may have hidden sources of water.

Death Valley

This is Death Valley, in the United States. The highest temperature ever recorded on the Earth's surface was measured here 100 years ago. It was an amazing 134°F (57°C). Temperatures rise so high because the air is very dry.

DID YOU KNOW?

In Death Valley, people sometimes say it's so hot you could "fry an egg on a car bonnet".

The heat can cause problems for visitors. People are warned to stay with their car if they break down and not to walk to find help. A car offers some shade from the sun and is easier for rescuers to spot. Outside, the glare of the sun reflected from the ground can cause eye problems – even blindness, if you don't shield your eyes.

The Outback

The central area of Australia is known as the Outback, or the "Red Centre". It is very hot and it hardly ever rains – sometimes just once a year.

The people who have lived here for tens of thousands of years are called Aboriginal people. They know how to find food and water in the vast desert. They can dig down into dry river beds, or extract water from roots and plants.

Aboriginal people tell stories to help them remember the places where water can be found. These stories are learned by children so that they know what to do if they are ever in trouble.

The Aboriginal people know that the roots of the kurrajong tree hold water in them. The roots can be peeled and crushed to make a life-saving drink.

A kurrajong tree

As well as being able to find water, what else do the Aboriginal people need in order to survive in the Outback?

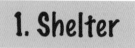

1. Shelter

They create shade from the sun during the heat of the day, by making simple shelters using branches.

DID YOU KNOW?

Desert creatures such as skinks survive by burrowing into the sand during the heat of the day, and coming out in the cool of the night. We can learn how to survive by watching what the local animals do.

2. Food

They use spears and **boomerangs** to hunt and kill animals, such as emus and wallabies.

They also know how to start a fire without matches, so they can cook the meat.

Would YOU be able to start a fire without matches?

boomerang a curved throwing weapon used by Aboriginal people for hunting

Ricky Megee

One person who survived in the Australian Outback was Ricky Megee.

In 2006, he walked out of the desert, having survived there for ten weeks. He had been driving in the northern desert when he was attacked by robbers. His car was stolen, and he was left for dead. He walked barefoot for ten days, shredding the soles of his feet, until he found a natural dam that held water.

Ricky made a shelter from the sun and survived by eating leeches and grasshoppers. He caught frogs and "cooked" them by threading them onto a wire and leaving them out in the heat of the sun. He also had to pull out his own rotten teeth. When found, he was described as a "walking skeleton" … but he was alive.

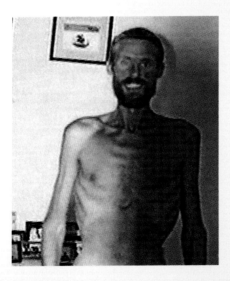

Ricky Megee photographed soon after his return from the Outback

SURVIVING AT
ALTITUDE

In high-up places, such as the Andes in South America, visitors are warned to watch out for the signs of **altitude** sickness. The first sign is usually a sudden bad headache. It is caused by a lack of oxygen in the air. Without enough oxygen, you can die.

The Andes in South America

altitude being very high above sea level

A few years ago, the presenters of the BBC's
Top Gear programme visited South America.
Jeremy Clarkson, James May and Richard
Hammond were trying to cross a high mountain
pass at over three miles above sea level.
They started suffering from altitude sickness and
had to head quickly down to a lower level.

The cars they were testing
managed to keep going.
It was the presenters
who couldn't cope
with the height!

High risk: Everest

Mount Everest is the world's highest mountain.

To reach the top, climbers have to enter the "death zone". This is the area above 8000 metres, where no one can survive for more than forty-eight hours. Over two hundred people have died on the mountain in the last hundred years.

Climbing a wall of ice on Everest

Climbers on Everest have to pass the bodies of others who died on earlier trips. They are frozen in place, close to the route. In some cases, climbers use them as "signposts" to tell them they are going the right way or have reached a certain point in the climb.

The bodies can't be taken away easily, because of the effort it takes to get to this height, and the cost of moving anything to or from the base camp, which is near the bottom of the mountain.

This is the body of George Mallory, who died while climbing Mount Everest in 1924. The body was found in 1999.

Surviving on Everest

Surviving on a very high mountain such as Mount Everest needs great strength. Climbers must be well equipped, well prepared and very fit. A period of calm weather is needed. This only happens for a few weeks each year.

FACT FILE

Mount Everest

Height: 8848 metres

First successfully climbed: 1953, by Sir Edmund Hillary and **Sherpa** Tenzing Norgay

Sherpa a person who lives in the area of Mount Everest

The summit of Everest

What may happen ...

The thin air means you may start "seeing things" and "hearing voices". Your face grows icy as your breath freezes in the cold. Your body starts to save heat by stopping the blood flowing to your hands and feet. This causes frostbite.

DID YOU KNOW?

The most dangerous mountain in the world is Annapurna in Nepal. It is the hardest to climb. Fewer than one hundred and fifty people have stood on its summit.

Joe Simpson

In the Andes of Peru there is a mountain called Siula Grande.

Two friends, Simon Yates and Joe Simpson, got into trouble here in 1985. They were the first people to climb the mountain's West Face and reach the summit. On their way back down, Joe fell. He smashed his right leg terribly.

Siula Grande in South America

The men were short of food and they knew that if Simon stayed to help, they would probably both die. As darkness fell, they tried to carry on, with Simon lowering Joe down on their ropes because he couldn't walk.

In the dark, Simon accidentally lowered Joe over a cliff. He didn't have the strength to pull him back up again. Both men were now stuck, and Simon was being dragged towards the edge. He decided that he had to cut the rope …

A scene from Touching the Void, *the film based on Joe Simpson's story of survival*

Simon spent the night in a snow shelter. In the morning, he looked over the cliff and thought his friend must be dead. It was a long drop and he couldn't see a body. He made his way back to their camp, very upset at the death of his friend.

But Joe was not dead.

He had fallen down a crack in the ice, but managed to make his way out. He crawled and dragged himself, in terrible pain, for six miles, following Simon's footsteps in the snow.

Even with a broken leg, Joe managed to lower himself into this ice cave and crawl to safety.

The journey took all his mental and physical strength. It was three days before he reached the tent, just as Simon was about to leave.

Simon couldn't believe Joe had survived. Joe then had to spend two days riding a mule to reach hospital and finally be treated.

Joe still goes climbing.

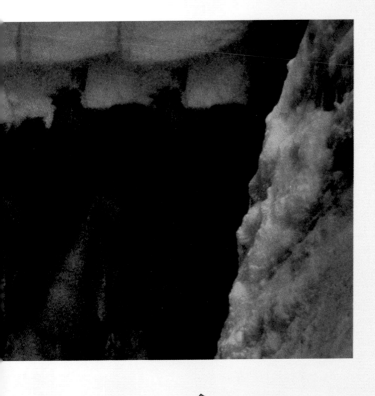

SURVIVING WITHOUT FOOD

Experts think it might be possible to survive for up to sixty days without food, but only if your body uses as little energy as possible.

Grub's Up!

Which of these insects can you eat?

1. Green ant

2. Cricket

3. Scorpion

4. Tarantula

Answers are on page 48.

Lost in the jungle

In 2007, two Frenchmen were walking in the Amazon jungle. They had planned to follow a trail and had enough food for twelve days. But they got lost in the jungle. They lit fires to try to attract attention, but they were hidden from view by the thick layer of leaves above them.

The men wandered for seven weeks, trying to find a way out. They had to eat centipedes, frogs and large spiders to survive before they finally found the trail.

One advantage of eating spiders is that everyone can have a leg!

DID YOU KNOW?

Another insect you can eat is the witchetty grub. It looks like a huge maggot. It tastes better when cooked: a bit like egg.

Flight 571

In October 1972, a plane carrying forty-five people crashed, high up in the snow and ice of the Andes mountains in South America.

Eighteen people died in the crash and in the next few days.

The survivors tried to shelter in the broken plane. They had to cope with extreme cold without winter clothes. Their shelter was also hit by an avalanche.

This photo of the survivors in the crashed plane was taken by their rescuers.

In the end, two of the strongest men were chosen to try to climb over a mountain and find help. This took them ten days.

The rest of the passengers were finally rescued. Altogether, they had been there for seventy-two days.

How had they survived without food for so long?

At first, they said they had found some cheese. In fact, they had eaten strips of flesh from the bodies of people who had died – some of whom were their friends.

LOST AND FOUND

If you're travelling somewhere, it's always best to plan your route and make sure people know where you are going. Stories often end badly because there was no route map – or because it wasn't followed.

This doesn't just happen on land. The sea is the world's largest wilderness, and a boat can be very hard to spot. Sailors now have **GPS**, so that their position can be tracked all the time.

Zachary Mayo

Zachary Mayo was a sailor serving on the ship the USS *America* in the Indian Ocean. In 1995 he fell overboard in an accident and no one realised at the time.

How did he survive?

He kicked off his boots, which would have weighed him down. Then he took his trousers off. He tied the bottoms and filled them with air so that he could float on them. He spent two nights floating before he was rescued by a passing fishing boat. He was very lucky, as he had no way of attracting attention.

GPS = global positioning system. It uses signals from satellites in space. If you have a GPS, you can always find out exactly where you are – anywhere in the world.

The San José miners

One of the greatest modern survival stories took place beneath the ground at the San José copper mine in Chile.

In August 2010, a tunnel collapsed, trapping thirty-three miners deep underground. For the first seventeen days, the miners didn't know whether they would ever be found. They survived on a few spoonfuls of tuna, sips of milk and water, and a biscuit every two days. They had no way of letting anyone know they were still alive.

Each day, at least one person would start to panic and needed to be calmed down. No one would have survived if the men hadn't taken care of each other.

Eventually, rescue workers managed to send down a narrow tube. The miners sent up a message to say they were all alive.

Supplies were then sent down the tube. Each package took an hour to reach the miners.

The miners spent another two months underground, while the tube was widened. Finally, after sixty-nine days, all the men were freed. Each miner had to squeeze into a small capsule for the fifteen-minute ride up to freedom.

Free at last

THE WILL TO SURVIVE

Most people who survive have a mental strength that keeps them going. The miners of San José had each other, but what about people who find themselves in trouble alone?

Could you survive danger and hardship alone?

On the next two pages are stories of two young people who found themselves in deadly danger far from help – and lived to tell the tale.

Aron Ralston

In 2005, Aron was climbing alone in a canyon in the United States. No one knew where he was. His arm was caught under a huge rock in an accident.

After being trapped there for several days, and after his water had run out, he realised there was only one way to escape. He would have to cut off his own arm, just below the elbow. He only had a penknife to do this, so it was a slow and very painful process.

He still goes climbing.

Juliane Koepcke

Seventeen-year-old
Juliane was on a flight
over the Amazon
jungle in 1971.
Lightning struck
the engine, and the
plane exploded. She
was the only survivor.

Her father had taught her to follow water
downhill. As she walked, she had to pass dead
bodies and wreckage. She went calmly past
crocodiles, and she waded through water
filled with piranha fish. The stream gave her
water, and she had sweets from the plane.
One of the cuts in Juliane's arm filled with
maggots from fly eggs. After ten days, she
found a canoe belonging to forest workers,
and was saved.

Survival quiz

In this book you've read about some of the terrible things that can happen to people. You've also learned about some true stories of survival.

Do you think you have what it takes to be a survivor? Try the quiz below to find out ...

1. If you're really hot in the desert, should you roll your sleeves up or down?

2. What is usually said to be the most important survival tool?

3. Which animal would you follow to lead you to water: a giraffe or a baboon?

4. In cold areas, matches should be left in a box with the striking ends sticking out – why?

Answers are on page 48.

Picture this ...

You are walking your dog in a woodland in winter, with deep snow on the ground. You walk deep into the woods and leave the main path.

Suddenly, you trip and roll down a steep bank and bang your head against a tree.

When you wake up, it is dark, you are cold and you find that your ankle is broken … You left your mobile phone at home.

What do you think you would do?

Reader challenge

Word hunt

 1 On page 7, find an adjective that means "bright and gleaming".

 2 On page 18, find a verb that means "digging a hole".

 3 On page 26, find an adjective that means "quiet and still".

Text sense

 4 What equipment is good for a survival kit? (page 8)

 5 What are people warned to do if their car breaks down in Death Valley? (page 15)

 6 What three key things do the Aboriginal people need in order to survive in the Outback? (pages 16–19)

 7 What happened to the *Top Gear* presenters when they visited South America? (page 23)

8 How do you think Simon Yates felt when he found out his friend Joe had survived? (pages 29–31)

Your views

9 How did the story of Juliane Koepcke make you feel? (page 43) Give reasons.

10 Which was the most interesting survival story? Give reasons.

Spell it

With a partner, look at these words and then cover them up.

- extreme
- explore
- expert

Take it in turns to read the words aloud. The other person has to try to spell each word. Check your answers, then swap over.

Try it

With a partner, read pages 28 to 31 again. Now imagine you are Simon Yates and Joe Simpson. Do a freeze-frame of the moment when Joe gets back to the tent, alive.

William Collins's dream of knowledge for all began with the publication of his first book in 1819. A self-educated mill worker, he not only enriched millions of lives, but also founded a flourishing publishing house. Today, staying true to this spirit, Collins books are packed with inspiration, innovation and practical expertise. They place you at the centre of a world of possibility and give you exactly what you need to explore it.

Collins. Freedom to teach.

Published by Collins Education
An imprint of HarperCollins*Publishers*
77-85 Fulham Palace Road Hammersmith London W6 8JB

Browse the complete Collins Education catalogue at **www.collinseducation.com**

Text by Alan Parkinson © HarperCollins*Publishers* Limited 2014

Series consultants: Alan Gibbons and Natalie Packer
10 9 8 7 6 5 4 3 2 1

ISBN 978-0-00-754614-5

British Library Cataloguing in Publication Data.
A catalogue record for this publication is available from the British Library.

Commissioned by Catherine Martin
Edited by Sue Chapple
Project-managed by Lucy Hobbs and Caroline Green
Proofread by Hugh Hillyard-Parker
Production by Emma Roberts
Picture research by Amanda Redstone
Design and cover design by Paul Manning
Printed and bound in China by South China Printing Co.

Answers

Page 10: Mittens keep the fingers together, so that they help to warm each other. **Pages 32–33:** They can all be eaten – though you might not want to! **Survival quiz, pp. 44–45: 1.** Keep your sleeves rolled down (as long as you are wearing light clothes), to reduce sweat loss from bare skin. This slows down the loss of water from your body. **2.** A knife. **3.** A baboon – it needs water, while a giraffe hardly ever drinks. **4.** If someone comes in with frostbitten hands, they may not be able to open the matchbox to light a fire.

Acknowledgements
The publishers would like to thank the students and teachers of the following schools for their help in trialling the Read On series:

Queensbury School, Queensbury, Bradford
Southfields Academy, London
Ormiston Six Villages Academy, Chichester

The publishers gratefully acknowledge the permission granted to reproduce the copyright material in this book. While every effort has been made to trace and contact copyright holders, where this has not been possible the publishers will be pleased to make the necessary arrangements at the first opportunity.

The publisher would like to thank the following for permission to reproduce pictures in these pages :

Cover image © Vitalii Nesterchuk/Shutterstock
Back cover image © Alexander Chaikin/Shutterstock

p. 5 Moviestore collection Ltd /Alamy, p. 5 AF Archive/ Alamy, p. 7 Diego Cervo/Shutterstock, p. 8 (left) Petr Salinger/Shutterstock, p. 8 (left) Garsya/Shutterstock,p. 8 (right) Volodymyr Krasyuk/Shutterstock, p. 9 (left) Winston Link/Shutterstock, p. 9 (right) Nata-Lia/ Shutterstock, p. 10 (left) Royal Geographical Society/ Alamy, p. 10 (right) Royal Geographical Society/Alamy, p. 12–13 Anton Foltin/Shutterstock, p. 14–15 Buena Vista Images/Getty Images, p. 16 Deco/Alamy, p. 17 ImageBroker /Alamy, p. 18 Bill Bachman/Alamy, p. 19 Roger Bamber/Alamy, p. 20 Totajla/Shutterstock, p. 21 Press Association Images, p. 22 to 23 Kastianz/ Shutterstock, p. 24 ImageBroker/Alamy, p. 25 Gamma Rapho/Getty Images, p. 27 Arsgera/Shutterstock, p. 28 Mikadun/Shutterstock, p. 29 Photos 12/Alamy, p. 31 AF Archive/Alamy, p. 32 (top left) Yongkiet jitwattanatam/ Shutterstock, p. 32 (top right) Dr. Morley Read/ Shutterstock, p. 32 (bottom left) Efendy/Shutterstock, p. 32 (bottom right) Linn Currie/Shutterstock, p. 33 Mr Suttipon Yakham/Shutterstock, p. 34 Everett Collection Historical/Alamy, p. 35 kastianz/Shutterstock, p. 36–37 JokerPro/Shutterstock, p. 39 Claudia Vega/ EPA/Corbis, p. 40 HO/Reuters/Corbis, p. 41 Dudarev Mikhail/Shutterstock, p. 42 Nora Feller/Corbis, p. 43 Bettmann/Corbis, p. 45 Ailisa/Shutterstock.